cupcakes
by colour

General manager Christine Whiston
Editorial director Susan Tomnay
Creative director & designer Hieu Chi Nguyen
Senior editor Stephanie Kistner
Food director Pamela Clark
Test Kitchen manager Belinda Farlow
Editorial assistant Elizabeth Hooper
Recipe development Nicole Jennings, Rebecca Squadrito,
Kirrily La Rosa

Director of sales Brian Cearnes
Marketing manager Bridget Cody
Business analyst Rebecca Varela
Operations manager David Scotto
Production manager Victoria Jefferys
International rights enquiries Laura Bamford
lbamford@acpuk.com

ACP Books are published by ACP Magazines
a division of PBL Media Pty Limited
Publishing director, Women's lifestyle Pat Ingram
Director of sales, Women's lifestyle Lynette Phillips
Commercial manager, Women's lifestyle Seymour Cohen
Marketing director, Women's lifestyle Matthew Dominello
Public relations manager, Women's lifestyle Hannah Deveraux
Creative director, Events, Women's lifestyle Luke Bonnano
Research Director, Women's lifestyle Justin Stone
PBL Media, Chief Executive Officer Ian Law

Photographer Stuart Scott
Stylist Vicki Liley
Cake preparation/decoration Nicole Jennings

The publisher would like to thank the following
for props used in photography:
Robert Gordon Australia; The Christmas Shop;
Highlands Miniatures.

Produced by ACP Books, Sydney.
Published by ACP Books, a division of ACP Magazines Ltd.
54 Park St, Sydney NSW Australia 2000.
GPO Box 4088, Sydney, NSW 2001.
Phone +61 2 9282 8618 Fax +61 2 9267 9438
acpbooks@acpmagazines.com.au www.acpbooks.com.au
Printed by SNP Leefung Printers, China.

Australia Distributed by Network Services,
GPO Box 4088, Sydney, NSW 2001.
Phone +61 2 9282 8777 Fax +61 2 9264 3278
networkweb@networkservicescompany.com.au
United Kingdom Distributed by Australian Consolidated Press (UK),
10 Scirocco Close, Moulton Park Office Village, Northampton, NN3 6AP.
Phone +44 1604 642 200 Fax +44 1604 642 300
books@acpuk.com www.acpuk.com
New Zealand Distributed by Southern Publishers Group,
21 Newton Road, Auckland.
Phone +64 9 360 0692 Fax +64 9 360 0695 hub@spg.co.nz
South Africa Distributed by PSD Promotions,
30 Diesel Road Isando, Gauteng Johannesburg.
PO Box 1175, Isando 1600, Gauteng Johannesburg.
Phone +27 11 392 6065/6/7 Fax +27 11 392 6079/80
orders@psdprom.co.za
Canada Distributed by Publishers Group Canada,
Order Desk & Customer Service,
9050 Shaughnessy Street, Vancouver, BC V6P 6E5.
Phone (800) 663 5714 Fax (800) 565 3770 service@raincoast.com

Title: Cupcakes by colour / food director Pamela Clark.
Publisher: Sydney: ACP Books, 2008.
ISBN: 978-1-86396-891-1 (pbk)
Notes: Includes index.
Subjects: Cupcakes.
Other authors/contributors: Clark, Pamela.
Also titled: Australian women's weekly.
Dewey number: 641.8653
© ACP Magazines Ltd 2008
ABN 18 053 273 546
This publication is copyright. No part of it may be reproduced
or transmitted in any form without the written permission of
the publishers.

To order books, phone 136 116 (within Australia).
Send recipe enquiries to: recipeenquiries@acpmagazines.com.au

THE AUSTRALIAN
Women's Weekly

cupcakes
by colour

acp
books

contents

introduction

Is there anyone who doesn't love cupcakes? These precious little offerings are just right for so many occasions from children's birthday parties, to elegant high tea or to serve as individual celebration cakes for weddings, engagements and special events. *Cupcakes By Colour* is a book of ideas for the most gorgeous cupcakes in the world. We've divided the chapters by colour: pink, white, yellow, blue/green and chocolate, but the beauty of this book it that you can adapt the decorations for these delightful little cakes and create any colour combination you like. Our aim is to show you how to decorate more than 100 cupcakes in simple and pretty ways using easy-to-buy sweets, lollies and decorations.

pink

jelly bean hearts

Top each cake generously with fluffy frosting. Cut an edge from one end of each small jelly bean, sandwich the cut ends together to make a heart-shape. Position hearts on the cakes before the frosting has set.

dreamy rainbows

Colour butter cream in varying shades of pinks and purples. Use small piping bags (without tubes) to pipe bands of colour on the top of each cake. Blend the colours slightly, using a spatula.

roses & romance

Spread the top of each cake with a generous layer of white chocolate ganache. Top each cake with a bought dried rose bud.

jaffa-topped

Colour butter cream pink. Spread the top of each cake generously with the butter cream. Top each cake with a jaffa.

chocolate truffle hearts

Colour butter cream pale pink. Spread the top of each cake with butter cream. Fit a small piping bag with a small fluted tube, half-fill the bag with butter cream. Pipe a shell pattern around the edge of each cake. Top each cake with an iced heart-shaped chocolate truffle.

swirl of hearts

Colour butter cream pink. Fit a large piping bag with a fluted tube, half-fill the bag with butter cream. Pipe a large swirl of butter cream on top of each cake. Sprinkle butter cream with pink and red edible sugar hearts. Twist a length of gem strings on wire around each cake.

coconut ice butterflies

Colour glacé icing pink. Working with one cake at a time, spread the top of each cake with glacé icing, then immediately dip each in desiccated coconut. When the icing is set, cut a round hole, about 1cm deep, in the top of each cake. Whip chilled thickened cream until it holds its shape. Halve the rounds of cake to make butterfly wings. Fill each hole with strawberry jam then the cream. Position the wings on the cakes.

valentine hearts

Colour a little fluffy frosting red. Half-fill a small piping bag (without a tube) with the red frosting. Spread white fluffy frosting on the top of each cake. Pipe three dots of the red frosting onto the unset white frosting. Pull a toothpick through each dot to make heart shapes.

mosaic magic

Colour butter cream pink. Spread the butter cream fairly thickly, but evenly, on the top of each cake. Decorate each cake in a mosaic pattern with pink lollies – we used Smarties, mini musks, small boiled lollies and sliced licorice cream rock logs. Fill in the gaps with pink cachous.

sour flowers

Colour butter cream pink. Fit a large piping bag with a large fluted tube, half-fill the bag with the butter cream. Pipe small swirls of butter cream on the top of each cake. Split spearmint leaf lollies in half horizontally, quarter strawberry-flavoured sour straps lengthways. Roll strips into spiral shapes, position on cakes with mint leaves. Position silver cachous in centre of flowers.

pink & pretty glitter

Fit a large piping bag with a large fluted tube, half-fill the bag with butter cream. Pipe a large swirl of butter cream on the top of each cake; spray with pink colour mist then sprinkle with pink edible glitter.

silver slipper

Colour butter cream lilac. Spread the top
of each cake evenly with the butter cream.
Place lavender sugar sprinkles into a shallow
dish, roll the edge of the top of each cake
in the sprinkles to make a border. Working
with one cake at a time, gently push a high
heel shoe cutter into the butter cream
in the centre of each cake. Fill inside the
cutter with a single layer of silver cachous;
gently push cachous into the butter cream.
Remove the cutter, ready for the next cake.

hugs & kisses

Colour butter cream pink. Spread the top
of each cake evenly with the butter cream.
Position sugar heart-shaped lollies on cakes
– in a cross for kisses and a circle for hugs.

berries & cream

Colour unwhipped chilled thickened cream pale pink. Whip the cream until it barely holds its shape. Top each cake with cream and a mixture of your favourite berries – we used blueberries, raspberries and strawberries. Dust the berries with a little sifted icing sugar.

hearts & arrows

Colour butter cream red. Spread the top of each
cake with the butter cream. Cut and trim chocolate-
coated mint sticks to make arrows, position on cakes.
Top cakes with red foil-covered chocolate hearts.

coconut cherry top

Fit a large piping bag with a large fluted tube, half-fill the bag with cream cheese frosting. Pipe a large swirl of the frosting on the top of each cake, sprinkle lightly with desiccated coconut, top with a maraschino cherry.

purple lollies galore

Fit a large piping bag with a large fluted tube, half-fill the piping bag with fluffy mock cream. Pipe a large star on the top of each cake. Top cream with mounds of purple lollies – we used halved jubes, small jelly beans, Smarties and fizzers. Finish the cakes with purple candles.

sparkly
baubles

Colour butter cream pink. Fit a large piping
bag with a fluted tube, half-fill the piping
bag with the butter cream. Pipe a generous
swirl of butter cream on the top of each cake.
Place edible lavender and white baubles on
butter cream.

pretty in purple

Spread the top of each cake evenly with butter cream. Working with one cake at a time, gently push a small (about 2cm long) leaf cutter into the butter cream, sprinkle some green sugar sprinkles inside the cutter, gently remove the cutter. Repeat this to make another leaf on the cake. Position purple edible sugar roses on cakes.

bunch of flowers

Spread the top of each cake evenly with butter cream. Make the stems for the flowers by cutting thin strips (about 3cm long) from green snakes. Tie a piece of ribbon around each bunch of stems, position on cakes. Position pink and white edible sugar flowers on cakes.

daisiness

Colour butter cream pink. Spread the top of each
cake fairly thickly, but evenly, with butter cream.
Position about six white Choc Melts around the
outside of each cake to make petals for the daisies,
use pink jelly buttons (ours were aniseed in flavour)
for the centre of the daisies.

sequin swirl

Fit a large piping bag with a large fluted tube, half-fill the bag with fluffy frosting. Pipe a large swirl of the frosting on top of each cake. Sprinkle cakes with edible sequins.

pink frangipani

Fit a large piping bag with a large fluted tube, half-fill the bag with fluffy mock cream. Pipe stars on the top of each cake. Cut white marshmallows in half horizontally, dip the sticky side of each half in pink sugar sprinkles, pinch one end of each half to make a petal shape. Use five halves to make each frangipani, use some more sugar sprinkles to fill in any white gaps on the marshmallows.

marbled magic

Colour half a batch of fluffy mock cream pink. Gently mix the pink mock cream with the white cream to give a marbled effect. Fit a large piping bag with a large plain tube (or use the bag without a tube), half-fill the bag with the marbled cream. Pipe the cream into mounds on the top of each cake, decorate with pink and silver cachous. Top cakes with edible sugar flowers.

white

toasty coconut

Stir coarsely flaked coconut in a frying pan over a low heat until it is browned lightly; remove from the pan immediately to cool. Spread the top of each cake generously with cream cheese frosting; sprinkle with the toasted coconut.

mallow moments

Use scissors to cut toasted coconut-covered marshmallows into small pieces. Spread the top of each cake fairly thickly with butter cream; top with marshmallow pieces.

silver cloud

Fit a large piping bag with a large fluted tube, half-fill the bag with cream cheese frosting. Pipe a generous swirl of the frosting on the top of each cake, sprinkle with fine silver sprinkles. Top cakes with large silver cachous.

white choc curls

Use a sharp vegetable peeler to make chocolate curls by shaving the curls from the side of a bar of white chocolate. Spread the top of each cake generously with white chocolate ganache, top with the chocolate curls.

silver anniversary

Colour butter cream white. Spread the top of each cake evenly with the butter cream. Position silver cachous on each cake to write 25, gently push the cachous into the butter cream.

pastel pink hearts

Brush the top of each cake with warmed sieved apricot jam. Tint some ready-made white icing pink. Roll double the amount of white ready-made icing (to the amount of pink) between sheets of baking paper until it is 5mm thick. Roll the pink icing between sheets of baking paper until 5mm thick. Cut rounds of white icing large enough to cover the top of each cake (about 7cm). Use a 3cm heart-shaped cutter to cut out heart shapes from the pink icing and from the centre of the white icing rounds. Remove the white heart shapes, replace them with the pink hearts. Roll the icing again, gently, between sheets of baking paper to ensure the hearts are in place. Position rounds on cakes.

baby booties

Colour cream cheese frosting white. Spread the frosting evenly over the top of each cake. Position edible sugar booties in the centre of each cake, decorate with clusters of pink cachous.

baby rattle

Cut bamboo skewers into 5cm lengths, secure three lengths together with sticky tape to make handles for the rattles. Wrap pink and blue ribbon around the handles to cover them; tie a bow around the top of each handle. Push the handles into Ferrero Raffaelo chocolate truffles. Spread the top of each cake with whipped white chocolate ganache, top with rattles.

wedding cakes aglow

Colour butter cream white. Fit a large piping bag with a large fluted tube, half-fill the bag with butter cream. Pipe generous swirls on the tops of the cakes, sprinkle with silver cake sparkles. Push wedding cake candles into the stars.

rings forever

Spread the top of each cake evenly with fluffy frosting. Position silver cachous on each cake to make ring shapes, gently push the cachous into the frosting before it sets. We decided we'd like to have a pink diamond engagement ring, but we settled for pink cachous.

sugared violets

Brush a tiny amount of unbeaten egg white all over the petals of freshly picked violets; sprinkle damp petals lightly with caster sugar, gently shake off any excess sugar. Dry the violets on a fine wire rack. Spread the top of each cake quickly with glacé icing. Position violets in the centre of each cake.

rose petals

Spread the top of each cake with glacé icing.
Position fresh rose petals in the centre of
each cake before the icing has set.

silver snowstorm

Dollop and swirl spoonfuls of fluffy frosting on the top of each cake. Sprinkle cakes with different sized silver cachous before the frosting has set.

dazzlers

Spread the top of each cake with glacé icing. Melt white Choc Melts, half-fill a small piping bag (without a tube) with the warm chocolate, quickly drizzle chocolate backwards and forwards over the set iced cakes. Quickly sprinkle cakes with small silver cachous before the chocolate has set.

sugared hearts

Use a hard plastic stencil which has varying sized and shaped hearts. Working with one cake at a time, place the stencil on the top of the cake, use a fine sifter to sift icing sugar over the cut-out shapes. Gently lift the stencil off the cake. Brush the excess icing sugar from the stencil before using on the next cake.

daisy mints

Spread the top of each cake with fluffy frosting. Use about six tic tacs to make the petals for each daisy, push the tic tacs gently into the frosting. Use tiny yellow flowers (from a jar of edible sugar "hearts and flowers") for the centre of the daisies.

pearls for girls

Colour butter cream white. Spread the top of
each cake with the butter cream. Gently push
oyster pearl cachous into the butter cream
in the shape of a strand of pearls. Use gold
cachous for the clasp.

first anniversary

Paper is the symbol for a first wedding anniversary; we've used ready-made soft icing to make a "paper" scroll.

Roll a small amount (about the size of a marble) of ready-made white icing on an icing-sugared board until it is 3mm thick. Cut a neat 5cm square from the icing. Roll the icing into a scroll shape, stand the scroll on a baking-paper-covered surface until firm. Make as many scrolls as you need. Colour butter cream white. Spread the top of each cake evenly with the butter cream. Position scrolls on the cakes. Use either tiny ready-made icing hearts, or, cut out hearts from scraps of the icing and leave them to dry, to use as "seals" on the scrolls. Secure hearts to the scrolls by brushing the backs of the hearts with a tiny amount of water.

snowflake sparkles

Melt some white Choc Melts. Half-fill a small piping bag (without a tube) with the melted chocolate. Pipe snowflake shapes onto baking paper, top each with a large oval silver cachous; leave the snowflakes to set at room temperature. Spread the top of each cake with a thick layer of fluffy frosting and sprinkle cakes with sparkling pearl sugar crystals. Position a snowflake on each cake before the frosting has set.

sweet & simple

Working with one cake at a time, spread the top of each cake with glacé icing. Position a sugar flower in the centre of each cake before the icing has set.

purple power

Fit a large piping bag with a large fluted tube,
half-fill the bag with fluffy frosting. Pipe a medium-
sized star on top of each cake. Position a purple
sugar flower in the centre of each cake before the
frosting has set.

fluffy frosted sprinkles

Fit a large piping bag with a large fluted tube, half-fill the bag with fluffy frosting. Pipe a generous swirl of frosting on the top of each cake. Sprinkle each cake with bright coloured sprinkles before the frosting has set.

butterflies

Whip chilled thickened cream until it barely holds its shape. Cut a round hole, about 3cm deep, in the top of each cake. Halve the rounds of cake to make butterfly wings. Fill each hole with strawberry jam, then the cream. Position the wings on the cakes. Dust cakes lightly with sifted icing sugar.

snowflakes

Dollop the top of each cake with a generous spoonful of fluffy frosting. Use a spatula to shape and swirl the "snow", sprinkle cakes with edible sugar snowflakes.

yellow

checkerboard

Colour butter cream white. Spread the top of each cake evenly with the butter cream. Remove orange fondant sections from licorice allsorts, cut each section into four squares. Make a checkerboard pattern on the cakes with the fondant squares.

dotty

Colour butter cream orange. Spread the top of each cake evenly with the butter cream. Position orange Smarties and orange mini M&M's on each cake.

fruity stripes

Spread the top of each cake evenly with butter cream. Halve yellow and orange fruit sticks crossways. Trim the ends of the fruit sticks to fit neatly on the top of each cake.

spirals

Colour butter cream lemon. Spread the top of each cake evenly with the butter cream. Make spirals, starting from the centre of the cake, using different sized yellow lollies – we used rainbow chips, then mini M&M's, then Smarties to create the spiral.

fruity citrus
wedges

Half-fill a large piping bag (without a tube) with
fluffy frosting. Pipe swirls of the frosting on top
of each cake. Position orange and yellow fruit
salad wedges on the frosting before it has set.

banana split

Fit a large piping bag with a large fluted tube, half-fill the bag with butter cream. Pipe a swirl of butter cream on the top of each cake. Top cakes with small white mallow bakes and banana lollies. Drizzle melted dark chocolate over the top of each cake, sprinkle with chocolate sprinkles.

ring of roses

Spread the top of each cake with butter cream. Position a circle of yellow and/or white sugar roses in the centre of each cake.

baby feet

Colour butter cream white. Spread the top of each cake evenly with the butter cream. Split small yellow jelly beans in half lengthways, position on cakes. Use yellow writing icing to pipe toes.

button-ups

Brush the top of each cake with a little warmed
sieved jam. Tint some ready made white icing
lemon. Roll pieces of the icing between sheets
of baking paper to about 5mm thick. Cut rounds
from the icing large enough to cover the top of
each cake (about 7cm). Position the rounds on
each cake. Use the blunt edge of a slightly smaller
round cutter to mark the edge of the buttons.
Make button holes from mini mints.

gift boxes

Colour butter cream yellow. Spread the top of each cake generously with the butter cream. Tie ribbon around licorice allsorts to make gifts. Position gift boxes in the centre of each cake.

baby carrot cakes

Fit a large piping bag with a large fluted tube, half-fill the bag with cream cheese frosting. Pipe a swirl of the frosting on the top of each cake. Sprinkle cakes with orange sprinkles, top with tiny edible sugar carrots.

lemon curd creams

Cut deep triangular holes into the top of
each cake; reserve lids. Whip thickened
cream until it holds its shape. Fit a large
piping bag with a large fluted tube, half-
fill the bag with the cream. Fill the holes
with lemon curd. Pipe cream over the curd,
drizzle with a little extra curd. Position lids in
the centre of each cake. Dust cakes with a
little sifted icing sugar.

gold star

Brush the top of each cake with warmed sieved apricot jam. Knead equal quantities of white and chocolate ready-made soft icing together to make a milk-chocolate-coloured icing. Roll the icing between sheets of baking paper to 1cm thick. Cut rounds from the icing large enough to cover the top of each cake (about 7cm). Cut a 5cm star shape from the centre of each round. Position the rounds on top of each cake. Fill the star shapes with a single layer of gold cachous.

dainties

Spread the top of each cake generously with butter cream. Remove green fondant sections from licorice allsorts. Cut out leaf shapes from the fondant, using either a 2cm leaf cutter or a sharp pointed vegetable knife. Top each cake with a leaf and an edible sugar flower.

mellow yellow

Fit a large piping bag with a large fluted tube, half-fill
the bag with butter cream. Pipe a large swirl on the
top of each cake, sprinkle with yellow sprinkles.

sunflower

Spread the top of each cake with a thick layer of butter cream. Position a row of candy corn around the outside edge of each cake, then position another row of the corn on the inside. Sprinkle some yellow sugar crystals in the centre of each cake.

spotty

Tint ready made white soft icing yellow. Roll an equal quantity of white soft icing (to the yellow) between sheets of baking paper until it is 5mm thick. Roll the yellow icing between sheets of baking paper until it is 5mm thick. Cut 2cm rounds, quite close together, from both pieces of icing. Place white rounds in the holes left in the yellow icing, and the yellow rounds in the holes left in the white icing. Roll both pieces of icing again, between sheets of baking paper to ensure the rounds are in place. Brush the top of each cake with a little sieved warm apricot jam. Cut rounds from each piece of icing large enough to cover the top of each cake (about 7cm). Position rounds on each cake.

daisy glaze

Working with one cake at a time, spread the
top of each cake with lemon glacé icing.
Position edible sugar flowers in the centre
of each before the icing has set.

stardust

Fit a large piping bag with a large fluted
tube, half-fill the bag with butter cream.
Pipe a large star on the top of each cake.
Slice orange and yellow fruit sticks
crossways, position on the butter cream.

banana &
passionfruit cream

Dollop generous spoonfuls of whipped
thickened cream on the top of each cake.
Place finely-sliced banana on top of the
cream then drizzle with passionfruit.

blue & green

minty snowflakes

Colour butter cream blue. Spread the top of each cake evenly with the butter cream. Gently push mini mints into the butter cream in the shape of snowflakes. Dust cakes with sifted icing sugar.

christmas baubles

Colour butter cream blue. Spread the top of each cake evenly with the butter cream. Outline the pattern for the baubles and the loop with blue cachous. Use blue edible glitter to fill in the pattern. Make a loop with a thin strip of licorice strap, gently push the loop into the butter cream and top with a white mallow bake.

christmas berries

Colour butter cream white. Spread the top of each cake with the butter cream. Split spearmint leaf lollies in half horizontally, gently push the leaves into the butter cream. Use jaffas to make the berries.

christmas wreaths

Colour butter cream white. Spread the top of each cake with a thick layer of the butter cream. Split spearmint leaf lollies in half horizontally, you'll need about six leaves for each cake. Gently push the halved leaves, smooth-side up and slightly overlapping, into butter cream in the shape of a wreath. Decorate leaves with silver and gold cachous.

blueberries
& cream

Top each cake with generous spoonfuls of
sweetened whipped thickened cream. Place
fresh blueberries on cream. Dust cakes with
finely sifted icing sugar.

sugared almonds

Spread the top of each cake with glacé icing. Position a blue sugared almond in the centre of each cake before the icing has set.

blue heaven

Spread the top of each cake with butter cream.
Position four or five edible blue sugar flowers on
the top of each cake.

starbright

Tint ready made white icing blue. Roll an equal quantity of white icing (to the blue) between sheets of baking paper until it is 5mm thick. Roll blue icing between sheets of baking paper until it is 5mm thick. Ues a 3cm star cutter to cut out star shapes, quite close together, from both pieces of icing. Place white stars in the holes left in the blue icing. (If you like, you can also place some of the blue stars in the holes left in the white icing – we used just the white stars.) Roll icing again, between sheets of baking paper, to ensure the stars are in place. Brush the top of each cake with a little sieved warmed apricot jam. Cut rounds from icing large enough to cover the top of each cake (about 7cm). Position rounds on each cake.

on top of the hill

Colour butter cream green. Colour desiccated coconut green by rubbing colouring into the coconut. Dollop a generous amount of butter cream on the top of each cake and shape into mounds; sprinkle with green coconut. Melt milk Choc Melts, half-fill a small piping bag (without a tube) with the chocolate. Pipe 40 (or whatever numbers suit you) onto a piece of baking paper, leave the numbers to set at room temperature. Push the numbers gently into the side of each butter cream mound.

peppermint
cream sundae

Colour butter cream green, then flavour
the cream with a little peppermint oil or
essence. Break up some Flake bars, and
stir through the butter cream. Dollop a
generous amount of butter cream on the
top of each cake then use a spatula to form
a scoop of ice-cream. Spoon some melted
milk Choc Melts over the butter cream then
sprinkle with more crumbled Flake before
the chocolate has set.

three of hearts

Colour fluffy frosting green. Use a 2cm heart cutter to cut out heart shapes from Mint Patties. Spread the top of each cake fairly thickly with the frosting. Position three hearts on each cake before the frosting has set.

mosaic magic

Spread the top of each cake fairly thickly with white chocolate ganache. Decorate each cake in a mosaic pattern with blue and green lollies – we used Lifesavers, mini M&M's, Skittles and baby jelly beans. Gently push the lollies into the ganache.

make a wish

Split white mallow bakes in half horizontally. Colour glacé icing blue. Working with one cake at a time, spread the top of each cake evenly with the glacé icing. Position five mallow halves for petals and a blue cachous in the centre, before the icing has set. Half-fill a small piping bag (without a tube) with royal icing, pipe the stems on the cakes after the icing has set.

glamour masks

Colour butter cream blue. Spread the top of each cake evenly with the butter cream. Make a mask shape on each cake using silver and blue cachous in a single layer. Push each cachous gently into the butter cream. Use sticks cut from lollypops for the handles of the masks. Use small pieces of ribbon and sugar flowers to cover and decorate the top of the handles.

blue crystals

Fit a large piping bag with a large fluted tube,
half-fill the bag with butter cream. Pipe large
swirls of butter cream on the top of each cake,
sprinkle with blue sugar crystals.

cute as a button

Colour butter cream white. Spread the top of each cake with the butter cream. Gently push six small green boiled Bo Peep lollies into the top of each cake to make flower shape. Place a brown Smartie in the centre of each flower.

chocolate

chocolate kisses

Whip white chocolate ganache until fluffy. Spread the top of each cake with ganache. Position milk chocolate kisses and small chocolate star sprinkles over cakes.

rainbows

Fit a large piping bag with a large fluted tube, half-fill the bag with dark chocolate ganache. Pipe generous swirls on the top of each cake. Decorate cakes with multi-coloured Smarties and rainbow chips.

peanut heaven

Marble some chunky peanut butter through milk chocolate ganache. Fit a large piping bag with a large fluted tube, half-fill the bag with the ganache mixture. Pipe generous swirls of the ganache on the top of each cake, sprinkle with crushed peanut brittle.

malt ganache

Fit a large piping bag with a large fluted tube, half-fill the bag with whipped milk chocolate ganache. Pipe generous swirls on the top of each cake. Decorate cakes with Maltesers, brown mini M&M's, gold cachous and gold edible glitter.

fairy lamingtons

Working with one cake at a time, dip the top
of each cake in chocolate glacé icing, then
immediately dip in desiccated coconut. When
the icing has set, cut a 3cm wide hole, about
1cm deep, in the top of each cake. Fill each
hole with double cream. Place the rounds on
each cake.

marbled
choc caramel

Spread the top of each cake with a fairly thick layer of dark chocolate ganache. Dollop about six small dots of caramel Top 'n' Fill on the ganache. Pull a skewer back and forth through the caramel for a marbled effect.

dragonfly

Spread the top of each cake with a thick layer of chocolate butter cream. Make the dragonfly bodies using about four white Choc Bits each. Cut big speckles (5.5cm) into quarters, position two quarters on each cake for wings. Use pieces of shredded coconut for antennae.

mochaflies

Spread the top of each cake evenly with mocha butter cream. Cut thin strips, about 3cm long, from licorice straps, position on cakes to make bodies and antennae of mochaflies. Cut milk and dark chocolate-coated coffee beans in half crossways, position, cut-side up, for wings.

imelda

Spread the top of each cake with white chocolate ganache. Attach small edible sugar butterflies to chocolate high-heeled shoes with tiny dabs of ganache. Position shoes on cakes.

chocky lips

Dollop the top of each cake with milk chocolate ganache, sprinkle with red cake sparkles. Top each cake with a pair of red lolly lips.

milkyway stars

Spread the top of each cake with a thick layer of dark chocolate ganache. Position milk chocolate stars on cakes.

magical
mushrooms

Spread the top of each cake with a thick layer
of dark chocolate ganache. Position white Choc
Melts and white Choc Bits on cakes.

music music

Melt some white Choc Melts. Half-fill a small piping
bag (without a tube) with the chocolate. Pipe treble
clefs and musical notes onto a baking-paper-lined
tray; set at room temperature. Spread the top of
each cake with a generous layer of milk chocolate
ganache. Cut thin strips from licorice straps,
position the strips on each cake to make staves.
Secure treble clefs and notes on the staves with
tiny dabs of ganache.

chocolate hearts

Dollop the top of each cake with generous spoonfuls of whipped milk chocolate ganache. Remove foil wrappers from chocolate hearts, gently push a heart into the ganache. Dust cakes with sifted cocoa powder.

marshmallow snowballs

Spread the top of each cake with an even layer of dark chocolate ganache. Position a coconut and chocolate-coated eskimo snowball on the cakes.

choc mint crush

Spread the top of each cake generously with dark chocolate ganache. Top each cake with crushed mint chocolate drops.

chocolate
easter eggs

Spread the top of each cake with whipped white chocolate. Position small chocolate easter eggs in the centre of each cake.

cakeuccinos

Spread the top of each cake evenly with fluffy mock cream. Working with one cake at a time, hold a cappuccino stencil closely to the top of the cake. Use fine sifter to sift cocoa powder over the cutout shape. Gently lift the stencil away from the cake. Brush the excess cocoa from the stencil before using on the next cake.

cross your heart

Spread the top of each cake evenly with dark chocolate ganache. Melt some white Choc Melts. Half-fill a small piping bag (without a tube) with the chocolate. Working with one cake at a time, pipe random criss-cross lines of chocolate across the cake. Position red sugar hearts on chocolate before it has set.

nest egg

Spread the top of each cake with a thick layer of
dark chocolate ganache. Break Flake bars into
pieces, push the pieces gently into the ganache to
make nests. Position blue sugared almonds in the
centre of each nest.

graduation

Spread the top of each cake with white chocolate ganache. Place a mint slice ball in the centre of each cake, position a square of chocolate on the mint ball to make a mortarboard. Cut thin strips, about 4cm long, from licorice strap, split the end of each strip into fine strips to make tassels. Attach a tassel to each mortarboard with a tiny dab of melted dark chocolate.

milk chocolate whip

Fit a large piping bag with a large fluted tube, half-fill the bag with whipped chocolate ganache. Pipe large swirls of the ganache on the top of each cake. Sprinkle with chocolate sprinkles.

cakes

Here's a selection of some of our favourite cupcake-friendly recipes. There's a rich, but easy fruit cake, old favourites like banana, carrot and butter cakes, a great quick-mix chocolate cake, a light-as-a-feather sponge cake and a good selection of cakes for people who have various allergies. Each hole in the standard muffin pan we used had a fluid capacity of ⅓-cup/80ml. The paper cases we used had a side measurement of 40mm (a little taller than those bought from supermarkets) and a base diameter of 48mm.

vanilla butter cakes

1 cup (150g) self-raising flour
90g softened butter
1 teaspoon vanilla extract
½ cup (110g) caster sugar
2 eggs
2 tablespoons milk

1 Preheat oven to 180°C/160°C fan-forced. Line eight holes of 12-hole muffin pan with paper cases.
2 Sift flour into small bowl, add butter, extract, sugar, eggs and milk; beat with electric mixer on low speed until ingredients are combined. Increase speed to medium; beat until mixture is changed to a paler colour.
3 Drop ¼ cup of mixture into cases. Bake about 20 minutes. Stand cakes 5 minutes before turning top-side up onto wire rack to cool.
Makes 8

sponge cakes

3 eggs
½ cup (110g) caster sugar
¼ cup (35g) cornflour
¼ cup (35g) plain flour
¼ cup (35g) self-raising flour

1 Preheat oven to 180°C/160°C fan-forced. Line 10 holes of 12-hole muffin pan with paper cases.
2 Beat eggs in small bowl with electric mixer about 5 minutes or until thick and creamy; gradually add caster sugar, one tablespoon at a time, beating until sugar dissolves between additions. Transfer to large bowl.
3 Meanwhile, sift dry ingredients twice, then sift over egg mixture; fold ingredients together.
4 Drop ¼ cup of mixture into cases. Bake about 25 minutes. Turn cakes immediately onto wire rack, then turn top-side up to cool.
Makes 10

quick-mix chocolate cakes

1 cup (150g) self-raising flour
½ cup (75g) plain flour
⅓ cup (35g) cocoa powder
¾ cup (165g) caster sugar
185g softened butter
3 eggs
½ cup (125ml) milk

1 Preheat oven to 180°C/160°C fan-forced. Line 15 holes of two 12-hole muffin pans with paper cases.
2 Sift dry ingredients into medium large bowl, add remaining ingredients; beat with electric mixer on low speed until ingredients are combined. Increase speed to medium; beat until mixture is smooth and has changed to a paler colour.
3 Drop ¼ cup of mixture into cases. Bake about 20 minutes. Stand cakes 5 minutes before turning top-side up onto wire rack to cool.
Makes 15

dark chocolate mud cakes

60g dark eating chocolate, chopped coarsely
⅔ cup (160ml) water
90g softened butter
1 cup (220g) firmly packed brown sugar
2 eggs
⅔ cup (100g) self-raising flour
2 tablespoons cocoa powder
⅓ cup (40g) almond meal

1 Preheat oven to 170°C/150°C fan-forced. Line 12-hole muffin pan with paper cases.
2 Stir chocolate and the water in small saucepan over low heat until smooth.
3 Beat butter, sugar and eggs in small bowl with electric mixer until light and fluffy. Stir in sifted flour and cocoa, meal and warm chocolate mixture.
4 Drop ¼ cup of mixture into cases. Bake about 25 minutes. Stand cakes 5 minutes before turning top-side up onto wire rack to cool.
Makes 12

caramel mud cakes

125g butter, chopped coarsely
100g white eating chocolate,
 chopped coarsely
⅔ cup (150g) firmly packed
 brown sugar
¼ cup (90g) golden syrup
⅔ cup (160ml) milk
1 cup (150g) plain flour
⅓ cup (50g) self-raising flour
1 egg

1 Preheat oven to 170°C/150°C
fan-forced. Line 12-hole muffin
pan with paper cases.
2 Stir butter, chocolate, sugar,
syrup and milk in small saucepan
over low heat until smooth.
Transfer mixture to medium
bowl; cool 15 minutes.
3 Whisk sifted flours into
chocolate mixture, then egg.
4 Drop ¼ cup of mixture into
cases. Bake about 30 minutes.
Stand cakes 5 minutes before
turning top-side up onto wire
rack to cool.
Makes 12

white chocolate mud cakes

125g butter, chopped coarsely
80g white eating chocolate,
 chopped coarsely
1 cup (220g) caster sugar
½ cup (125ml) milk
½ cup (75g) plain flour
½ cup (75g) self-raising flour
1 egg

1 Preheat oven to 170°C/150°C
fan-forced. Line 12-hole muffin
pan with paper cases.
2 Stir butter, chocolate, sugar
and milk in small saucepan over
low heat until smooth. Transfer
mixture to medium bowl; cool
15 minutes.
3 Whisk sifted flours into
chocolate mixture, then egg.
4 Drop ¼ cup of mixture into
cases. Bake about 30 minutes.
Stand cakes 5 minutes before
turning top-side up onto wire
rack to cool.
Makes 12

rich fruit cakes

90g softened butter
½ cup (110g) firmly packed
 brown sugar
2 eggs
1 tablespoon orange
 marmalade
2⅓ cups (375g) mixed dried
 fruit, chopped finely
⅔ cup (100g) plain flour
2 tablespoons self-raising flour
1 teaspoon mixed spice
2 tablespoons sweet sherry
1 tablespoon sweet sherry,
 extra

1 Preheat oven to 150°C/130°C
fan-forced. Line eight holes
of 12-hole muffin pan with
paper cases.
2 Beat butter, sugar and eggs
in small bowl with electric
mixer until combined; transfer
mixture to medium bowl. Stir
in marmalade and fruit.
3 Stir in sifted dry ingredients
and sherry.
4 Drop ⅓ cup of mixture into
cases. Bake about 1¼ hours.
Brush cakes with extra sherry.
Cover pan with foil; cool cakes
in pan.
Makes 8

banana cakes

125g softened butter
¾ cup (165g) firmly packed
  brown sugar
2 eggs
1½ cups (225g) self-raising flour
½ teaspoon bicarbonate of soda
1 teaspoon mixed spice
1 cup mashed overripe banana
½ cup (120g) sour cream
¼ cup (60ml) milk

1 Preheat oven to 180°C/160°C
fan-forced. Line 16 holes of
two 12-hole muffin pans with
paper cases.
2 Beat butter and sugar in small
bowl with electric mixer until
light and fluffy. Beat in eggs,
one at a time.
3 Transfer mixture to large bowl;
stir in sifted dry ingredients,
banana, sour cream and milk,
in two batches.
4 Drop ¼ cup of mixture into
cases. Bake about 30 minutes.
Stand cakes 5 minutes before
turning top-side up onto wire
rack to cool.
Makes 16

carrot cakes

1 cup (250ml) vegetable oil
1⅓ cups (300g) firmly packed
  brown sugar
3 eggs
3 cups firmly packed,
  coarsely grated carrot
1 cup (110g) coarsely
  chopped walnuts
2½ cups (375g) self-raising flour
½ teaspoon bicarbonate of soda
2 teaspoons mixed spice

1 Preheat oven to 180°C/160°C
fan-forced. Line 18 holes of
two 12-hole muffin pans with
paper cases.
2 Beat oil, sugar and eggs in
small bowl with electric mixer
until thick. Transfer mixture to
large bowl; stir in carrot and
nuts, then sifted dry ingredients.
3 Drop ¼ cup of mixture into
cases. Bake about 30 minutes.
Stand cakes 5 minutes before
turning top-side up onto wire
rack to cool.
Makes 18

lemon poppy seed cakes

⅓ cup (50g) poppy seeds
¼ cup (60ml) milk
185g softened butter
2 teaspoons finely grated
  lemon rind
1 cup (220g) caster sugar
3 eggs
1½ cups (225g) self-raising flour
½ cup (75g) plain flour
½ cup (60g) almond meal
½ cup (125ml) orange juice

1 Preheat oven to 180°C/160°C
fan-forced. Line 12-hole muffin
pan with paper cases.
2 Combine seeds and milk in
small bowl, stand 20 minutes.
3 Beat butter, rind and sugar
in small bowl with electric mixer
until fluffy; beat in eggs one
at a time. Transfer mixture to
medium bowl; stir in sifted flours,
meal, juice and milk mixture,
in two batches.
4 Drop ⅓ cup of mixture into
cases. Bake about 35 minutes.
Stand cakes 5 minutes before
turning top-side up onto wire
rack to cool.
Makes 12

marble cakes

125g softened butter
1 teaspoon vanilla extract
⅔ cup (150g) caster sugar
2 eggs
1¼ cups (185g) self-raising flour
⅓ cup (80ml) milk
pink food colouring
1 tablespoon cocoa powder
2 teaspoons milk, extra

1 Preheat oven to 180°C/160°C fan-forced. Line 12-hole muffin pan with paper cases.
2 Beat butter, extract, sugar and eggs in small bowl with electric mixer until fluffy. Stir in sifted flour and milk in two batches.
3 Divide mixture among three small bowls. Tint one mixture pink. Blend sifted cocoa with extra milk in cup; stir into another bowl of mixture. Leave the third bowl of mixture plain.
4 Drop alternate spoonfuls of mixtures into cases. Pull a skewer through mixtures for a marbled effect. Bake about 20 minutes. Stand cakes 5 minutes before turning top-side up onto wire rack to cool.
Makes 12

ginger buttermilk cakes

½ cup (110g) firmly packed
   brown sugar
½ cup (75g) plain flour
½ cup (75g) self-raising flour
¼ teaspoon bicarbonate of soda
1 teaspoon ground ginger
½ teaspoon ground cinnamon
¼ teaspoon ground nutmeg
90g softened butter
1 egg
¼ cup (60ml) buttermilk
2 tablespoons golden syrup

1 Preheat oven to 170°C/150°C fan-forced. Line nine holes of 12-hole muffin pan with paper cases.
2 Sift dry ingredients into small bowl; add remaining ingredients. Beat mixture with electric mixer on low speed until ingredients are combined. Increase speed to medium; beat until mixture is changed to a paler colour.
3 Drop ¼ cup of mixture into cases. Bake about 35 minutes. Stand cakes 5 minutes before turning top-side up onto wire rack to cool.
Makes 9

flourless choc hazelnut cakes

¼ cup (25g) cocoa powder
¼ cup (60ml) hot water
100g dark eating chocolate,
   melted
100g butter, melted
1 cup (220g) firmly packed
   brown sugar
¾ cup (75g) hazelnut meal
3 eggs, separated

1 Preheat oven to 180°C/160°C fan-forced. Line nine holes of 12-hole muffin pan with paper cases.
2 Blend cocoa with the water in medium bowl until smooth. Stir in chocolate, butter, sugar, meal and egg yolks.
3 Beat egg whites in small bowl with electric mixer until soft peaks form; fold into chocolate mixture in two batches.
4 Pour ⅓ cup of mixture into cases. Bake 1 hour 10 minutes. Stand cakes 5 minutes before turning top-side up onto wire rack to cool.
Makes 9

gluten-free butter cakes

200g softened butter
2¼ cups (300g) gluten-free
  self-raising flour
1 cup (220g) caster sugar
½ cup (125ml) milk
2 eggs
2 egg whites

1 Preheat oven to 180°C/160°C fan-forced. Line two 12-hole muffin pans with paper cases.
2 Beat butter in medium bowl with electric mixer until changed to a paler colour.
3 Meanwhile, sift the flour with ¼ cup of the sugar, beat flour mixture and milk into butter, in two batches, until combined.
4 Beat eggs and egg whites in small bowl with electric mixer until thick and creamy. Gradually add remaining sugar, beating until dissolved between additions. Gradually beat egg mixture into flour mixture on a low speed.
5 Drop 2½ level tablespoons of mixture into cases. Bake about 20 minutes. Stand cakes 5 minutes before turning top-side up onto wire rack to cool.
Makes 24

gluten-free mandarin cakes

4 small mandarins (400g)
2 cups (280g) macadamias
250g softened butter
1 cup (220g) caster sugar
3 eggs
1 cup (170g) polenta
1 teaspoon gluten-free
  baking powder

1 Cover whole mandarins in medium saucepan with cold water; bring to the boil. Drain; repeat process twice. Cool.
2 Preheat oven to 180°C/160°C fan-forced. Line 18 holes of two 12-hole muffin pans with paper cases.
3 Blend or process nuts finely.
4 Halve mandarins; discard seeds. Blend mandarins until pulpy.
5 Beat butter and sugar in small bowl with electric mixer until light and fluffy. Beat in eggs, one at a time. Transfer mixture to large bowl; stir in polenta, baking powder, nuts and mandarin.
6 Drop ¼ cup of mixture into cases. Bake about 25 minutes. Stand cakes 5 minutes before turning, top-side up, onto wire rack to cool.
Makes 18

dairy-free chocolate cakes

125g dairy-free spread
100g dark eating chocolate
  (70% cocoa solids),
  chopped coarsely
¾ cup (180ml) soy milk
¾ cup (165g) caster sugar
1 cup (150g) self-raising flour
½ cup (75g) plain flour
2 tablespoons cocoa powder

1 Preheat oven to 150°C/130°C fan-forced. Line 12-hole muffin pan with paper cases.
2 Combine spread, chocolate, milk and sugar in medium saucepan; stir over low heat until smooth. Transfer to large bowl; cool 10 minutes. Whisk in sifted flours and cocoa until smooth.
3 Pour ¼ cup of mixture into cases. Bake about 25 minutes. Stand cakes 5 minutes before turning top-side up onto wire rack to cool.
Makes 12

frostings & finishes

All of the cupcakes in this book have a topping of some sort, from the simplest glaze through to lavish ganache. It's up to you to decide on the number of the cupcakes to make, and the type and amount of frosting you need to finish the cakes. Here are all the icings, frostings etc., we've chosen to use in this book, but let your imagination loose and do your own thing with different cake and frosting combinations. There are variations within the recipes to broaden your choices. In butter-based recipes, such as Butter Cream and Fluffy Mock Cream, we prefer to use unsalted butter – there is a little difference in the taste. Make sure you have the butter at room temperature, not melted or too hard; it's important to beat the butter until it is as white as possible for the best results. You can buy white colouring from cake decorator's suppliers if you need to whiten a butter-based icing. Pure icing sugar is best for royal icing and makes a good glaze for cakes, but regular soft icing sugar is adequate for everything else. Store-bought soft icing or fondant is a great product, and easy to use. Use colourings sparingly at first, until you determine their strength.

butter cream

Add any flavoured essence or extract you like to butter cream. Beat it in with the butter for the best flavour. Any citrus rind can be used. Beat 2 teaspoons finely grated rind with the butter and use the corresponding juice instead of the milk. Butter cream is the most popular type of frosting, it's easy to spread and handle. Be aware that it's cream in colour, so any added colouring will result in the final colour being slightly yellow, particularly pinks and reds.

125g butter, softened
1½ cups (240g) icing sugar
2 tablespoons milk

1 Beat butter in small bowl with electric mixer until as white as possible; beat in sifted icing sugar and milk, in two batches.
Makes 1¾ cups

variations
chocolate Sift 2 tablespoons cocoa powder with the sugar.
mocha Warm 1 tablespoon of the milk, stir in 2 teaspoons instant coffee granules, add the remaining tablespoon of milk. Sift 2 tablespoons of cocoa powder with the sugar.

ganache

Ganache can be made with milk, dark or white eating-quality chocolate. The methods are the same, but the amount of chocolate varies slightly, as do the resulting quantities. Ganache can be used while still warm and pourable, or it can be beaten with a wooden spoon until spreadable. If you want the ganache lighter and fluffier – referred to as whipped ganache – beat the cooled mixture in a small bowl with an electric mixer.

milk chocolate
½ cup (125ml) cream
200g milk eating chocolate, chopped coarsely
Makes 1 cup

dark chocolate
½ cup (125ml) cream
200g dark eating chocolate, chopped coarsely
Makes 1 cup

white chocolate
½ cup (125ml) cream
360g white eating chocolate, chopped coarsely
Makes 1½ cups

1 Bring cream to the boil in a small saucepan; remove from heat. When bubbles subside, add chocolate; stir until smooth.

glacé icing

Quick and easy, glacé icing is worth learning to make properly. You can alter the flavour, texture and colour easily. The butter (you can use vegetable oil instead) keeps the icing slightly soft, so it cuts well. Without the butter or oil, the icing tends to shatter. It's important that the icing only be warm, not hot, while it's being stirred over the pan of water – it will crystallise if over-heated.

2 cups (320g) icing sugar
1 teaspoon butter
2 tablespoons hot water, approximately

1 Sift icing sugar into small heatproof bowl; stir in butter and enough of the hot water to make a thick paste. Place bowl over small saucepan of simmering water; stir until icing is spreadable.
Makes 1 cup

variations
chocolate Sift 2 teaspoons cocoa powder with the sugar.
coffee Dissolve 1 teaspoon instant coffee granules in the water.
mocha Sift 2 teaspoons cocoa powder with the icing sugar, and dissolve 1 teaspoon instant coffee granules in the hot water.
passionfruit Stir in 1 tablespoon passionfruit pulp.

royal icing

Royal icing begins to set as soon as it's exposed to the air, so keep the icing covered tightly with plastic wrap while you're not working with it. Once the icing has dried, it will set hard, and when it's cut, it will shatter. But, it's great for piping, colouring, spreading and making snowy mounds.

1½ cups (240g) pure icing sugar
1 egg white
½ teaspoon lemon juice

1 Sift icing sugar through a very fine sieve. Lightly beat egg white in small bowl with an electric mixer; add icing sugar, a tablespoon at a time. When icing reaches firm peaks, use a wooden spoon to beat in juice; cover tightly with plastic wrap.
Makes 1 cup

cream cheese frosting

For a citrus flavour, beat 2 teaspoons finely grated orange, lemon or lime rind with the butter and cream cheese. This frosting goes particularly well with carrot and banana cakes. Like butter cream, it is very user-friendly, but takes colourings slightly better than butter cream.

30g butter, softened
80g cream cheese, softened
1½ cups (240g) icing sugar

1 Beat butter and cheese in small bowl with electric mixer until light and fluffy; gradually beat in sifted icing sugar.
Makes 1¼ cups

fluffy frosting

If you don't have a candy thermometer, boil the syrup until it's thick with heavy bubbles. Remove from heat, let bubbles subside, then reassess the thickness of the syrup. Once the frosting is made, you can spread it for quite a while before it begins to set and lose its gloss developing a meringue-like crust. It's perfect for colouring and piping.

1 cup (220g) caster sugar
⅓ cup (80ml) water
2 egg whites

1 Combine sugar and the water in small saucepan; stir over heat, without boiling, until sugar is dissolved. Boil, uncovered, without stirring, about 5 minutes or until syrup reaches 116°C on a candy thermometer. Syrup should be thick but not coloured. Remove syrup from heat, allow bubbles to subside.
2 Beat egg whites in small bowl with electric mixer until soft peaks form. While motor is operating, add hot syrup in a thin stream; beat on high speed about 10 minutes or until mixture is thick.
Makes 2½ cups

lemon glaze

This glaze is used when you want that soft dreamy opaque look on a cake, use any strained fruit juice you like in place of the lemon juice – be aware that the glaze will take on the colour of the juice – or just use water instead. The glaze needs to be poured and spread quickly while it is warm, as it begins to set as soon as it starts to cool.

1 cup (160g) pure icing sugar
1 tablespoon lemon juice, approximately

1 Sift icing sugar into small heatproof bowl; stir in enough strained juice to give a thick pouring consistency.
2 Stir icing over small saucepan of simmering water until thin enough to make a spreadable opaque glaze.
Makes ½ cup

fluffy mock cream

This frosting is whiter, lighter and fluffier than butter cream, and colours better too. Use any extract or essence you like to flavour the frosting.

2 tablespoons milk
⅓ cup (80ml) water
1 cup (220g) caster sugar
1 teaspoon gelatine
2 tablespoons water, extra
250g butter, softened
½ teaspoon vanilla extract

1 Combine milk, the water and sugar in small saucepan; stir over low heat, without boiling, until sugar is dissolved. Sprinkle gelatine over extra water in cup, add to pan; stir syrup until gelatine is dissolved. Cool to room temperature.
2 Beat butter and extract in small bowl with electric mixer, until as white as possible. While motor is operating, gradually pour in cold syrup; beat until light and fluffy. Mixture will thicken on standing.
Makes 2 cups

dairy-free chocolate frosting

This frosting is easy to handle, rich and luscious, and perfect for people who can't tolerate dairy products, it's a good substitute for ganache.

50g dairy-free spread
2 tablespoons water
¼ cup (55g) caster sugar
¾ cup (120g) pure icing sugar
2 tablespoons cocoa powder

1 Combine spread, the water and caster sugar in small saucepan; stir over low heat until sugar dissolves.
2 Combine sifted icing sugar and cocoa in medium bowl; gradually stir in hot spread mixture until smooth. Cover; refrigerate 20 minutes. Using wooden spoon, beat frosting until spreadable.
Makes ¾ cup

ready-made white icing

This icing, also known as fondant, is available from supermarkets, delis and cake decorating suppliers in various colours and flavours, including chocolate. Knead the icing on a surface lightly dusted with icing sugar until it loses its stickiness. Roll the icing out to the required thickness with a rolling pin on a surface lightly dusted with icing sugar, or roll between sheets of baking paper. Keep any icing you're not working with completely airtight by wrapping in foil or plastic wrap. Ready-made icing can be used for covering the tops of cakes, for moulding, or for cutting out various shapes, which will dry out at room temperature and hold their shape. You'll be surprised how easy it is to work with; it colours perfectly and the finish looks professional.

decorations

Simple, witty, unique – its the decoration that transforms a frosted cupcake into a show stopper. We used chocolates and lollies in all shapes and sizes, sugared flowers, candles, patterned powder and coloured paper cases, to create our individual little cakes.

1 Sugared almonds
2 Mini mints
3 Mini musks
4 Jubes
5 Fruit salad wedges
6 Small boiled lollies (Bo Peeps)
7 Standard paper cases
8 Red lip lollies
9 Lifesavers
10 Skittles
11 Small jelly beans
12 Fizzers
13 Candy Corn
14 Strawberry Sour Strap
15 Fruit sticks
16 Pearl candles
17 Wedding cakes candles
18 Dried rose buds
19 Snakes
20 Cappuccino stencils
21 Tic Tacs
22 Yellow writing icing
23 Maraschino cherries
24 Various sugar flowers
25 Sugar carrots
26 Various shaped cutters
27 Gem strings
28 Peanut brittle
29 Sugar booties
30 Jelly buttons
31 Spearmint Leaves
32 Bananas
33 Licorice Cream Rock Logs
34 Licorice Strap
35 Licorice Allsorts
36 Various sprinkles, cachous & sugar shapes
37 Iced Chocolate Truffles
38 Ferrero Raffaelo chocolate truffles
39 Jaffas
40 Cake sparkles
41 Edible glitter
42 Mint Chocolate Drops
43 Maltesers
44 Mini M&M's
45 Eskimo Snowball
46 Raspberry & vanilla marshmallows
47 Chocolate Kisses
48 Various chocolate-coated coffee beans
49 Smarties
50 Mint Slice Balls
51 Rainbow Chips
52 Mallow Bakes (mini marshmallows)
53 Toasted coconut marshmallows
54 Heart chocolates (foil wrapped)
55 Milky Way magic stars
56 Chocolate shoes
57 Mint Pattie
58 White & dark Choc Bits
59 White & dark Choc Melts
60 Flake bar
61 Chocolate easter eggs
62 Choc-mint Sticks
63 Lindt chocolate squares
64 Big Speckles

glossary

almond meal also called ground almonds.

baking powder, gluten-free used as a leavening agent in bread, cake, pastry or pudding mixtures. Suitable for people having an allergic response to glutens or seeking an alternative to everyday baking powder.

bicarbonate of soda also called baking soda.

butter use salted or unsalted (sweet) butter.

buttermilk originally the term given to the slightly sour liquid left after butter was churned from cream, today it is commercially made similarly to yogurt. Sold alongside fresh milk products in supermarkets. Despite the implication, it is low in fat.

chocolate

dark eating made of cocoa liquor, cocoa butter and sugar.

Melts small discs of compounded dark, milk and white chocolate ideal for melting and moulding.

milk eating most popular eating chocolate, mild and very sweet; similar in make-up to dark, but with the addition of milk solids.

white eating contains no cocoa solids but derives its sweet flavour from cocoa butter. Very sensitive to heat.

cocoa powder also known as unsweetened cocoa.

coconut

desiccated concentrated, dried, unsweetened and finely shredded coconut flesh.

shredded unsweetened thin strips of dried coconut flesh.

toasted flaked dried flaked coconut flesh purchased already toasted. Available from health food stores.

cornflour also known as cornstarch. Available made from corn or wheat.

eggs we use large chicken eggs weighing 60g. If recipes call for raw or barely cooked eggs, exercise caution if there is a salmonella problem in your area, particularly for children and pregnant women.

flour

plain also known as all-purpose.

self-raising all-purpose plain or wholemeal flour with baking powder and salt added; can be made at home by sifting flour with baking powder in the proportion of 1 cup flour to 2 teaspoons baking pwder.

food colouring vegetable-based substance available in liquid, paste or gel form.

gelatine a thickening agent. We used powdered gelatine; is also available in sheets known as leaf gelatine.

golden syrup a by-product of refined sugarcane; pure maple syrup or honey can be substituted.

hazelnut meal is made by grounding the hazelnuts to a coarse flour texture.

macadamias native to Australia; fairly large, slightly soft, buttery rich nut. Should always be stored in the fridge to prevent their high oil content turning them rancid.

milk we use full-cream homogenised milk unless stated otherwise.

top 'n' fill caramel a canned milk product made of condensed milk that has been boiled to a caramel.

mixed dried fruit a combination of sultanas, raisins, currants, mixed peel and cherries.

mixed spice a classic mixture generally containing caraway, allspice, coriander, cumin, nutmeg and ginger; cinnamon and other spices can be added.

peppermint oil from the peppermint plant; often used as a flavouring.

polenta also called cornmeal; a flour-like cereal made of dried corn (maize); also the name of the dish made from it.

poppy seeds small, dried, bluish-grey seeds of the poppy plant, with a crunchy texture and a nutty flavour. Available whole or ground in most supermarkets and delicatessens.

ready made white icing prepared fondant; available in supermarkets. See also page123.

sugar

brown a very soft, fine granulated sugar retaining molasses for its characteristic colour and flavour.

caster also known as superfine or finely granulated table sugar.

icing also known as confectioners' sugar or powdered sugar; pulverised granulated sugar crushed together with a small amount of cornflour.

pure icing also called confectioners' sugar or powdered sugar.

vanilla extract obtained from vanilla beans infused in water; a non-alcoholic version of essence.

vegetable oil a number of oils sourced from plant rather than animal fats.

index

conversion chart

measures

One Australian metric measuring cup holds approximately 250ml; one Australian metric tablespoon holds 20ml; one Australian metric teaspoon holds 5ml.

The difference between one country's measuring cups and another's is within a two- or three-teaspoon variance, and will not affect your cooking results. North America, New Zealand and the United Kingdom use a 15ml tablespoon.

All cup and spoon measurements are level. The most accurate way of measuring dry ingredients is to weigh them. When measuring liquids, use a clear glass or plastic jug with the metric markings.

We use large eggs with an average weight of 60g.

dry measures

METRIC	IMPERIAL
15g	½oz
30g	1oz
60g	2oz
90g	3oz
125g	4oz (¼lb)
155g	5oz
185g	6oz
220g	7oz
250g	8oz (½lb)
280g	9oz
315g	10oz
345g	11oz
375g	12oz (¾lb)
410g	13oz
440g	14oz
470g	15oz
500g	16oz (1lb)
750g	24oz (1½lb)
1kg	32oz (2lb)

liquid measures

METRIC	IMPERIAL
30ml	1 fluid oz
60ml	2 fluid oz
100ml	3 fluid oz
125ml	4 fluid oz
150ml	5 fluid oz (¼ pint/1 gill)
190ml	6 fluid oz
250ml	8 fluid oz
300ml	10 fluid oz (½ pint)
500ml	16 fluid oz
600ml	20 fluid oz (1 pint)
1000ml (1 litre)	1¾ pints

length measures

3mm	⅛in
6mm	¼in
1cm	½in
2cm	¾in
2.5cm	1in
5cm	2in
6cm	2½in
8cm	3in
10cm	4in
13cm	5in
15cm	6in
18cm	7in
20cm	8in
23cm	9in
25cm	10in
28cm	11in
30cm	12in (1ft)

oven temperatures

These oven temperatures are only a guide for conventional ovens. For fan-forced ovens, check the manufacturer's manual.

	°C (CELSIUS)	°F (FAHRENHEIT)	GAS MARK
Very slow	120	250	½
Slow	150	275-300	1-2
Moderately slow	160	325	3
Moderate	180	350-375	4-5
Moderately hot	200	400	6
Hot	220	425-450	7-8
Very hot	240	475	9